HONEY POTLUCK KIDS
ALPHABET TREE

BRYAN L SMITH

Order this book online at www.trafford.com
or email orders@trafford.com

Most Trafford titles are also available at major online book retailers.

Trafford PUBLISHING®   www.trafford.com
North America & international
toll-free: 844 688 6899 (USA & Canada)
fax: 812 355 4082

Our mission is to efficiently provide the world's finest, most comprehensive book publishing service, enabling every author to experience success. To find out how to publish your book, your way, and have it available worldwide, visit us online at www.trafford.com

Library of Congress Control Number:
978-1-6987-0901-7 (sc)
978-1-6987-0903-1 (hc)
978-1-6987-0902-4 (e)

Print information available on the last page.

Trafford rev. 08/11/2021

BIBLICAL ADDITION
Written By Bryan L Smith

Aa

A is for Adam, Adam was the first human God created.

Bb

B is for Bethlehem, Bethlehem is where Jesus was born.

Cc

C is for Christian is a person who follows Jesus Christ.

Dd

D is for David
King David was
the son of Jesse.

Ee

E is for Eve
Eve was the
first woman God
created.

Ff

F is for
Forbidden fruit
Adam and Eve
ate an apple from
the tree.

Gg

G is for God
God created
Heaven and the
Earth.

Hh

H is for Heaven
Heaven is where
God and
his Angels live.

Ii

I is for Isaiah
Isaiah was a
Jewish prophet.

Jj

J is for John the Baptist,
John baptized
Jesus Christ.

Kk

K is for Kenan, Kenan lived for 910 years

Ll

L is for Light,
Jesus is the light
of the World.

Mm

M is for Mary,
Mary was the
mother of Jesus.

Nn

N is for Noah, Noah built the Ark that saved the Animals.

Oo

O is for Omar, Omar was the great-great-grandson of Abraham.

Pp

P is for Paul,
Paul was an
Apostle who
taught the gospel.

Qq

Q is for Quartus Quartus he was stoned for preaching the gospel.

Rr

R is for Ruth, Ruth was the great-grand mother of King David.

Ss

S is for Samuel, Samuel he also Anointed the first two Kings of Israel.

Tt

T is for Thomas, Thomas was one of the twelve Apostles of Jesus Christ.

Uu

U is for Uzziah,
Uzziah became
King at the age
of 16, he reigned
52 yrs.

Vv

V is for Veil,
the Veil was torn
when Christ died
on the cross.

Ww

W is for Wisemen, 3 came bearing gifts for Baby Jesus.

Xx

X was a secret symbol used by Christians to indicate their membership

Yy

Y is for Years, Christ lived on earth about thirty-three years.

Zz

Z is for Zion,
Zion is the land
of Israel and the
city of Jerusalem

This book is dedicated to my aunt
CONNIE BURRIS
She was truly a Honey Potluck Kid.

These Kids are sweet as can be and they
all bring something different to the table.

REACH OUT:
Smithbryan64@yahoo.com

Printed in the United States
by Baker & Taylor Publisher Services